MEDITATIVE
PRAYERS FOR TO-DAY

ADAM BITTLESTON

THE CHRISTIAN COMMUNITY PRESS

TO ARTHUR AND VIOLET NEWTON

IN GRATITUDE

AND TO ALL PATIENT READERS

First Edition, Christmas 1953
Second Edition, Whitsun 1956
Third Edition, Easter 1960
Reprinted
Fourth Edition, Christmas 1966

Fifth Edition, April 1975

ISBN 0 900285 00 1

PRINTED PHOTOLITHO IN GREAT BRITAIN
BY EBENEZER BAYLIS AND SON, LTD.
THE TRINITY PRESS, WORCESTER, AND LONDON

CONTENTS

INTRODUCTION

LEARNING to pray is a life-long task. For most people of the present time, there are many doubts and uncertainties to be met. We look out into a world of overwhelming remoteness in space, and think of a past and a future reaching through vast periods of time; what meaning can the trivial voices possess, with which we try to speak to a Power behind all this immensity?

To this question we can receive the beginning of an answer comparatively soon. If we try to meditate, dwelling upon something which we have chosen as the mid-point of our inner attention—perhaps words that seem to us wise, or a memory which we can contemplate in a steady, receptive mood—the definite impression may be given to us that we are not alone with these thoughts, but that other beings are gazing down into our consciousness. They are sensitive to our thoughts and feelings, as we are aware of sights and sounds in the external world. Our attempts at prayer help to develop in us a sense of community with these invisible, helpful observers.

But in order to grow out of a triviality of mood and make ourselves more worthy to come into their field of vision, there should be in all our prayers an objective, contemplative element. We do not rush straight to our own personal wishes; if these are to enter at all, it must be because we have prepared them to take a right place in a greater context.

Every need or hope of ours can be seen in proportion, if we can see it in relation to the deeds of Christ. What we can learn about Him, if we see it in the right inner light, can lead us towards Him as He is now and for ever, as the greatest of invisible companions, through Whom the ultimate Ground of existence can truly be divined as Father.

Not only through the Gospels do we find help in approaching Christ inwardly. All the rhythms of Nature are teachers about Him. His enduring Will can be felt in the alternation of day and night, in the course of spring, summer, autumn and winter. Even what seems an arbitrary human rhythm, the seven-day week, has its great significance. For the Jews this was the reflection of the cosmic rhythms of creation; for the pagan the days were once guarded by the seven planetary deities. Among the Christians, the first day of the week, which commemorated for the Jew the creation of light, and for the pagan was under the guardianship of the Sun, received a new and ultimate consecration from the deed of Easter.

Never has it been more necessary for men to grow in response to the cosmic rhythms, and to feel them as a revelation of Christ, than at the present. To help in this is one of the fundamental purposes of the Christian Community, the religious movement founded in 1922 under the guidance of Rudolf Steiner. In the sacramental life of the Christian Community, groups of people in many countries find their way towards the companionship of Christ, feeling Him as Lord and Redeemer of nature as well as of man. Through the selflessness of a shared and living ritual, the most complete victory over all uncertainties about the reality of prayer can be achieved.

In the Christian Community, the personal life of devotion is left to the free initiative of its members. The personal prayers contained in this book were written in the course of thirty years' work in the Christian Community; and they are offered only as the suggestions of an individual to other individuals, wherever they may be, who may find any part of them useful. To read them all at once would be the surest way of making them meaningless. The reader may find one or two which he can best connect with his own thoughts. Of these, he can test each word in his mind—has it for him a real meaning, or does it at least hold out the hope, that it will acquire this with use? Could he substitute another word or name? A user of the Friday prayer, for example, to whom St. Columba or St. Elizabeth of Hungary were rather remote figures, could well substitute men or women nearer to him. But there may also be familiar words, which remind him too strongly of ideas and feelings in which he is no longer at home, and which have to be rescued or altered.

In the different editions of this book, a few changes have been made, with the hope of expressing better what was meant. Readers may not always think the changes well-advised, if they make the comparison, and may well prefer to keep what they know. At the present time, an attempt to express spiritual realities in words is faced with every kind of difficulty.

And yet human language originated and developed not simply from the needs of practical communication but through contact between man and spiritual beings greater than himself. All words that we now use in meditative prayer need to be restored to life by a renewal of this contact, in mindfulness of their origin.

July, 1966.

EVENING

I GO into the realm of the invisible.
The weight of my earthly body
The surging forces of my earthly life
Release their hold.
In the world into which I now enter
The watchful care of the Angels
The loving guidance of the Archangels
The creative power of the Spirits of the Ages
Work upon the souls of men.
My heart bears in it many thoughts of conflict,
But also the thought of Christ.
May this grow in the world of sleep
Into full being—
That I receive through powers of Light
His strength and peace.

MORNING

I come from the realm of the invisible,
And penetrate anew
The stream of my earthly life,
The house of my earthly body.
I thank the world of Spirit,
Which has held my soul.
I thank the world of earth,
Which has guarded my body.
May the Light of Christ
In the light of day
Shine for my soul
Upon paths of earth.
May the holy aims of God
Which have warmed my soul in sleep
Be remembered through the aid of Christ
In waking deeds.

SUNDAY

BEFORE the world's beginning
Christ's glory shone.
In the realm of eternity
He is with the Father,
Light of all true lights.
He came on earth
Taking the form of man,
Bearing the fate of man,
Lifting the burden of man.
Thou who hast overcome death
Strengthen our souls.
Let the eye of our spirit
Be raised towards Thee,
The giver of blessing.
In Thy sight may we stand.

MONDAY

When we go out into the world as we have made it
Everywhere there speaks to us
Forgetfulness of the Spirit.
If human work were to be without love
The earth would become a bleak and barren desert.
Through forgetfulness of the Spirit
Love ebbs away.
Bring to mind in us, O Christ,
Inspirer of true human love,
How we have come to the earth
From the fields of light,
From the heights of the Spirit.
May we bring to the earth
What we have seen in the Spirit.
May remembrance of God
Grow strong in our souls
Overcoming the mists
Which hide from us the purpose
In the work of each day.

TUESDAY

As light unites all beings of the world
So speech unites man and man.
But our speech today is heavy with guilt,
Guilt of indifference and unawareness,
Guilt of anger and pride.
Thy word, O Christ, encountered these;
They condemned Thee.
They live still in our word.
From our inmost hearts, O Christ,
Make new our speech.
When we speak with one another
May we remember
That we come from the Father,
And are led by Thee
To the awakening of the Holy Spirit,
Through the days and the weeks and the years.

WEDNESDAY

Upon the temple of man's body
Worked through the ages
The servants of God,
Mighty spiritual creators.
This is now my dwelling;
But it is darkened
By the power of tempters
To whom my soul has listened.
O Christ, against Thee
The voice of temptation
Could achieve nothing.
Thou art the Healer
For all man's sickness.
Work in this body
That each of its elements,
Its warmth and its breath,
Its quickening blood,
The bones which sustain
The form which God gave,
Be hallowed by Thee.

THURSDAY

O CHRIST, Thou readest
The living book of human destiny.
In all who come to Thee
Thou knowest the inmost soul,
The body's need, the spirit's seeking.
In my thought of human beings
May I receive Thy light.
In my experience of human deeds
May I feel Thy will.
May we all, as Thy Community,
Find the right ways
For human souls
Who will to serve Thy Spirit.

FRIDAY

LET me remember the servants of Christ,
Who kept in their hearts
His will for the world.
Beneath the Cross, the beloved disciple
Winning from pain eternal patience,
Beholding in darkness the new beginning.
Paul, who endured all persecution,
Rejoicing in the freedom of the Christian soul.
Columba, through the dark and the cold,
Journeying to build a faithful brotherhood.
Francis, overcoming the fear of leprosy,
And raising men's vision to the beauty of earth.
Elizabeth, bringing red roses
Into the depths of need.
The work of the servants of Christ
Holds in it sure promise
For the future of earth.
May we protect
What they have planted.
Their power live
In words and deeds of ours.

SATURDAY

O CHRIST, I remember with love and thankfulness
Those I have known
Who have passed through the gate of death.
I know that some of these have looked on my soul
From the realm in which their souls dwell.
I thank Thee for all I have received from them;
For Thou art Lord of human destiny.
May my thoughts and feelings reach unto them,
    through Thee;
May they add warmth and purpose
To my earthly life.
And may my meeting again with them
Be blessed by Thee.

EASTER I

UNTO the sorrowing heart of Mary Magdalene
Thou camest in the garden of fresh life
That seeks in flower and tree the sunlit air.

Unto the questioning head of Thomas Didymus
Thou camest in the quiet upper room
By barred doors sheltered from the city's hatred.

Unto the faltering will of Simon Peter
Thou camest on the lake shore where he laboured
As fisher with his brethren on the waters.

And so Thou comest to our sorrowing heart
In the pure rhythms of the earth, sun, stars—
Linking our being's pulse to Paradise.

And so Thou comest to our questioning head
Revealing how the slain and buried Good
Takes on new body from the Invisible.

And so Thou comest to our faltering will,
Speaking to each of us our own true name,
Calling us from our graves to work with Thee.

ASCENSION

THE clouds receive
The Risen Christ
That He may rule
The world of Life.

Witness of Him
We seek in earth
Where waters bear
The spirit's grace.

The moving air
And songs of birds
Say in the light
He has a home.

And blossoms feel
The loving flame
He sendeth them
As messengers.

Between men's hearts
Strengthen the love—
O Lord of bread,
Giver of wine!

That in the world
Thou fillest now
As Spirit-Sun
We lift our sight!

WHITSUN

Thou holy fire, making Thy home in us,
When we at peace can see and serve the truth,
Make strong in us the memory of Christ,
Bring to our tongues His world-renewing word.

Thou gracious light, uniting distant men
In certainty on paths of active thought,
Make clear to us the charge of destiny,
Bring to our heads Thy world-renewing hope.

Thou healing breath, who in the body's depths,
Restorest harmony with heaven's will,
Let live in us the order of the stars,
Bring to our hearts the world-renewing joy.

ST. JOHN THE BAPTIST
(Midsummer)

Thou herald spirit, by the Father's grace
Abiding witness to the Light of men,
Look on our seeking.

All we have done on earth has left its trace,
And all we say sounds on for spirit ears.
Help at our judging.

Baptizer of the waking soul, lead out
Our lives from barren conflict in the dark
Into Christ's presence.

Let sound the music of thy faithful heart,
Prophet of days to come, for brother men,
Unto Christ's glory.

AUGUST

Upon fields and orchards
Growing towards harvest
There look with blessing
The spirits of heaven;
And their gaze searches
Men's hearts for ripening.
In the close weaving
Of manifold fates
They feel the pattern.
To the great Weaver,
The Lord of destiny,
We send our thoughts.
He heals in the body
The senses' dullness.
He wakes in the soul
The spirit's will.
May His Community
Work in the world
Warmed by His grace—
Joining the sundered
Where at the altar
The ways of men meet.

SEPTEMBER

INTO the ripening
Of earth's great gifts
The mists of autumn
Begin to be woven.
We feel the touches
Of winter's coming.
The gentle earth
Has suffered conflict
Of man with man.
Dust is the witness
Of faithless hearts,
Of cruel thoughts.
May we learn
To care for the earth
Through the purpose of Michael,
Lord of the starry iron,
And the help of Raphael
Spirit of the morning dew.

MICHAELMAS I

Amid the storm of the world,
In which our souls share,
We seek the leader of the Angel-host,
Michael, who casts down the Dragon.
Into our thoughts may come through him
The sense of gentle awe,
Of patient reverence for the hidden wisdom
That is in all things.
And in our acts his courage
Will overcome the cramping fear
Which makes a slave of man.
Michael calls, when autumn darkens earth;
He leads to Christ, and fights for Christ, for ever;
So may we follow him, and fight beside him
Against the Dragon with enduring fire.

[The name of Michael is three syllables, which
mean "Who is like God?"]

MICHAELMAS II

WE need in the light of our day
The eternal Light of the Word of God.
When we seek with our thoughts this Light
On the path which leads from the cave
Where thinking and seeing are shadows,
Into the fields of life
Into the freedom of the heart—
We shall meet Michael
Who reveals how Christ
Awakens thinking
That it may serve God.

We need in the life of our day
The eternal Bread of the Word of God.
When we seek with our hearts this Bread
On the path which leads from the swamp
Where feeling is dulled,
Into the heights of Grace,
Into the realm of the Sun—
We shall meet Michael
Who reveals how Christ
Awakens feeling
That it may serve God.

We need in the soul of our day
The eternal Wine of the Word of God.
When we seek with our faith this Wine
On the path which leads from the desert
Where the beasts are raging,
Into the world of angels,
Into the will of the Spirit—
We shall meet Michael
Who reveals how Christ
Awakens willing
That it may serve God.

We need in the strife of our day
The eternal Peace of the Word of God.
Seeking this Peace with our whole being
On the path which leads from the nightmare
Of endless chaos,
Into the order of heaven
And to the Father of all things—
We shall meet Michael
Who reveals how Christ
Awakens Man
That he may serve God.

NOVEMBER

Lord among the seven candles!
Giver of the light undarkened!
Helper of the souls who struggle
With their passions' bitter visage
On the wide stairs of the Night—

Thou who bearest from the Father
Sun-Life changeful and unchanging,
Healing for the spirit's weakness
When it weaves from wandering shadows
Error that denies Thy Being—

Christ whose love calls forth the roses
From the cross on which we suffer;
Guardian of the door to Heavens
Where the deeds on earth unfinished
Through God's grace prepare fulfilment—

Thy strong soul unite our feeling
With the souls of men who journey
From the earth to distant star worlds;
And with those who seek the entry
To the earth which Thou hast hallowed.

ADVENT

THOU mothering earth
Hast received the live seed
Into the dark
Good shelter of soil.
The mantle of night
Thrown wide over us,
And the sun as it goes
Its swift and short journey,
Speak to our hearts
In warning and promise.
Thou Earth hast borne up
The footsteps of Mary
Journeying patiently
Southwards to Bethlehem;
And the Earth bears us
Today in our travail,
That we may bring forth
Christ in our spirit.
So we may await Him
Sent by the Father,
Healer and bringer
Into our being
Of the true gold.

CHRISTMAS

Voices in thunder from the bounds of heaven
Through age on age prepared the world of earth
To hold the form of man, whose inmost soul
Is born to serve the Christ.

His glory is about the humble child
Laid in the manger, bringing Paradise
New among men who lift their hearts to see
The gift beyond all thought.

Bless Thou our troubled souls, grown poor in love,
From Thy eternal mercy, which brings back
All that is lost into the fold of God,
O Word of worlds made man!

EPIPHANY

In grace there streams from starry heights
Heaven's compassion for mankind.
The holy tree of life within,
Unfolds its leaves to feel your touch.

Substance of wisdom, living gold,
Glows in our thankful thoughts of Christ.
And clouds of incense lift our prayer
To meet with joy the Spirit's will.

May we so live that in our deeds
Some part of all the healing strength
Which Christ has brought from stars to earth
May work like myrrh to mend the world.

FEBRUARY

He who walked the paths of Galilee,
And the streets of Jerusalem,
Is now among men
Over all the earth
Though our eyes may not see Him.
He shares man's grief,
He suffers man's conflict,
He breathes man's hope.
He seeks disciples
Who trust what can be seen
When the heart's light opens.
May we receive from Him
The life that sustains
Grace in the soul.
May He speak in our conscience
When we take up our work.
May He be our shepherd
When in the hours of sleep
We move in the Spirit.

LENT

BLIND is the soul
Imprisoned deep
In weary flesh.

And spirit-will
Is wrenched away
From living good.

But we may tread
The road the Christ
Did follow then;

When all the wrong,
And all the pain
Were gathered up

That He, the Lamb,
Might bear for man
The bitter load,

And meet with man
The prince of hell
In the soul's night.

EASTER II

By His strong thought forgetfulness of God,
By His strong love the hatred of the good,
By His pure life the bitterness of death,
Are overcome in depths of earth.

Time is no longer empty, through His deed;
In our heart's beat His living grace awakes;
Into our house the Easter air is breathed
With joy that heals our blood.

Thou makest new man's being that from God
Has made the long descent into the dark;
And as immortal brother Thou hast joined
The way of sons of men.

EARTH

SPIRITS of the Heights
Have sent their messengers:
Stones under our feet.
Upon the sustaining earth
May we be upright.

Spirits of the Heights
Have sent their messengers:
Flowers and trees around us.
Upon the living earth
May our hearts waken.

Spirits of the Heights
Have sent their messengers:
Birds and beasts about us.
Of all earth's offspring
May we be guardians.

Spirits of the Heights
Have sent their messengers:
Light and dark, life and death.
In all earth's changes
Christ may we find.

AGAINST FEAR

MAY the events that seek me
Come unto me;
May I receive them
With a quiet mind
Through the Father's ground of peace
On which we walk.

May the people who seek me
Come unto me;
May I receive them
With an understanding heart
Through the Christ's stream of love
In which we live.

May the spirits which seek me
Come unto me;
May I receive them
With a clear soul
Through the healing Spirit's Light
By which we see.

INTERCESSORY PRAYER

Thou angel who keepest watch
Over the destiny of . . .
Through waking and sleeping,
And the long ages of time:
May my thoughts, filled with hope,
Reach to him through thee.
May he be strengthened
From the founts of will
Which bear us towards freedom.
May he be illumined
From the founts of wisdom
Which warm the inmost heart.
May he feel peace
From the founts of love
Which bless men's work.

IN THOUGHT FOR A CHILD

In thy breath the light of the sun
In thy bread the salt of earth
In thy ears true words of love
Sustain thy growing, changing life;
That thy spirit's will may work
That thy soul be warmed by joy
That thy body's world be built.

FOR ONE WHO HAS DIED

The Good Shepherd lead thee
Where thou art transformed
That thou mayest breathe
The air of eternal Being.

Where thou workest as soul
For worlds to come
The grace of the Spirit
Unite us with thee.

A PRAYER FOR BRITAIN

O CHRIST, Thou knowest
The souls and spirits
Whose deeds have woven
This island's destiny.

May we who today
Are bearers of this destiny
Find the strength and the light
Of Thy servant Michael.

And our hearts be warmed
By Thy blessing, O Christ,
That our deeds may serve
Thy work of world healing.

THANKSGIVING

For the speaking light of the senses
Which bears into our souls
The world's abundance
I thank the powers of heaven.

For the health that is in our bodies
Even in illness and need
Sustaining, renewing, refreshing,
I thank the will of Christ.

For the wonders of human friendship
Which bless the life of earth
With the hope of eternal being
I thank the Father's love.

A NOTE ON
THE LORD'S PRAYER

IF anyone finds his way completely into the use of
the Lord's Prayer, he may well feel that no other
prayer is necessary for him. Every present need of
mankind, and all hopes for the future, are contained
within it. But we are not always able to use it
effectively. It is possible to approach it with all
sincerity and yet meet with considerable difficulty;
and it is possible to use it for years, and then find that
we have somehow lost touch with its meaning.

Above all we need to bear in mind that the words
of the Lord's Prayer are given to us by Christ Himself, and that each of them should be used as part of
His language—as belonging in the context of what
He said then to mankind, and of what He says now.
If any words or sentence of the Lord's Prayer is life-
less to us, we need to understand and feel it afresh,
by relating it to the fundamental purposes which
Christ has for humanity; for we can learn what these
purposes are.

We can think, for example, of three great qualities,
which human beings can consciously train and
develop in themselves: the capacities for wonder,

compassion and conscientious action. Rudolf Steiner spoke particularly of these qualities as providing instruments for the effective work of Christ upon the earth; and we can see from experience that this is so.

One possible way in which we can deepen and renew our relationship to the Lord's Prayer is by considering how the fulfilment of the petitions contained within it depends upon the development within humanity of these three qualities.

The Name of God can only be hallowed in the hearts of men through their power of wonder. If the world is dominated by a kind of knowledge which fails to awaken enough reverence, then the Name of God will be given meanings which are too narrow and personal. Nature and history have to be seen and known in ways which reach through the surface of things to the Divine creative work; only through this can human speech be purified in the way implied by the Lord's Prayer.

The Kingdom of God will come about through the development of genuine mutual compassion, in which is included the desire to protect each other's freedom. Within every community, small or great, to which we may belong, there is the opportunity to share in the development of this compassion, through which the joy of one can become everyone's joy, and the grief of one can become everyone's grief, without any intrusion into individual privacy. Today when we care deeply for another person, we often find it difficult not to urge them in directions which we think will be for their good; but we can look forward to the development of a mood within Christian communities through which it will become natural to wait for the maturing, within each individual, of his own freely given inner law, in the sense described in the Sermon on the Mount.

Held together by mutual compassion, and moved by compassion for the needs of the world as a whole, true communities can begin to fulfil the Will of God, "as it is in heaven, so also on the earth". The ultimate guide here is the voice of conscience; not anything derived from convention or outer influences, but the speech of that part of our being which is born "not of blood, nor of the will of the flesh, nor of the will of man, but of God". The Will of the Father is done where the true needs of every creature, for which He has made room in the world, are respected and fulfilled.

In the following three petitions, practical fields are

described in which these great aims can be served. Where conscience works, all kinds of Bread, everything that nourishes the being of man, will be rightly shared. We should not rely on governments to see that this happens; the vigilance of each individual, both for his immediate environment and for the remotest parts of the world, is needed. We can see how this sort of concern is gradually becoming accepted as natural in our time.

Through compassion, we can hope to learn the difficult art of forgiveness towards other men, and thereby open ourselves to receive the creative forgiveness which continually streams to us from heaven, through the course of our earthly destiny.

The words, "Lead us not into temptation", are often felt as a peculiar difficulty in the Lord's Prayer. "Temptation" is the testing of our spiritual purpose under the pressure of our wishes and emotions. We can indeed be led into this testing if we trust too much to our own personal powers of resistance; or if, allowing wishes to master us, we have to experience something of the darkness into which they would eventually lead. The power of wonder leads us in the opposite direction, away from the violence of desire; showing us the greatness of what is already being given, it teaches patience towards the wishes that are yet unfulfilled.

But it is possible for man to make a fundamentally different choice. He can reject wonder, compassion and conscience, and let himself be filled instead with the will to destroy. Something of this will lurks in nearly all men, generally very much disguised, for instance as apathy or despair. It is "the Evil", of which the last petition speaks. Complete inner freedom is only possible when the soul is no longer in any danger of being possessed by evil. Just as the Gospels describe in the Mother of Jesus the new Eve, in whose soul temptation can take no hold, so in the Beloved Disciple is indicated the human being in whose "I" the will to betray or deny can find no place. He has gone through the death of the jealous, assertive, everyday self and received his true, innermost Self from Christ. "Deliver us from the Evil" asks that this process of redemption at the very centre of man's being may happen more and more.

The whole of the Lord's Prayer can be experienced like a sunrise. But it is not simply the earth receiving light from outside; the earth itself begins to become radiant, in sevenfold glory. Any particular thoughts which we use to help us in bringing the words of the

Prayer to life are in the end to vanish within the flood of healing, gentle Light, into which we are led. Here the word "we" can itself be given for the first time its complete meaning. Its use before has only been shadowy and provisional.

It is the task of all meditative prayer to prepare us for the falling away of illusion—to the accomplishment here on earth of St. Paul's hope: "For now we see in a glass darkly, but then face to face. Now I know in part; then I shall understand fully even as I have been fully understood." The heaven, of which the Lord's Prayer says that it is the home of the Father, is not only above and beyond all that we experience on earth; it is also within everything we know, as the glory of the Father's understanding, in which He would have us share.